St. Ambrose
On Virginity

St. Ambrose
On Virginity

St. Ambrose
On Virginity

© Lighthouse Publishing 2018

All rights reserved. Without limiting the rights under copyright reserved above, no part of this publication may be reproduced, stored in a retrieval system, or transmitted, in any form or by any means (electronic, mechanical, photocopying, recording or otherwise), without the prior written permission of the copyright owner of this book.

Published by
Lighthouse Christian Publishing
SAN 257-4330
5531 Dufferin Drive
Savage, Minnesota, 55378
United States of America

www.lighthousechristianpublishing.com

The Books Concerning the Virgins.

Introduction

THE state of Virginity is undoubtedly commended in holy Scripture, both by our Lord and St. Paul, but learned men have differed in their opinions as to the original customs and rules observed by virgins in the earliest ages. Some suppose that from the very beginning it was the custom for them to make a solemn profession of the virgin life, and to live together in common. Others consider that their vows were private, and they lived sometimes together, sometimes in the homes of their parents. Others, again, believing that there was no more than a simple purpose on the part of the virgins signified by the veil, and the simplicity of their dress, attribute the first commencements of community life to St. Ambrose himself.

The first opinion is hardly tenable as regards any profession which was notorious. Statements in the earlier Acts of Martyrs are to be regarded with suspicion, as so much of this class of writings is spurious. The utterances also of Fathers and Councils hardly establish anything on this point more than on the second mentioned above.

There would seem to have been some who publicly, like Marcellina, the sister of St. Ambrose, made their profession, and formally received the veil at the hands of the Bishop; and others, equally steadfast in purpose, whose vow of virginity was made in private. Of the former, those living in Milan hardly seem to have led a life in common, but at Bologna [I. 60] they did. The terms, vow, taking the veil, and profession, were in use in St. Ambrose's day, as at present.

It would appear, then, that from the days of the apostles there were some who devoted themselves to God in a life of chastity, and that later on the promise or vow was made in the presence of others—the bishop, clergy, and friends. These virgins lived at home with their parents, whilst the times of persecution endured, making it practically impossible for them to live elsewhere. Common life amongst them would seem to have commenced in the East, and St. Athanasius, when, seeking refuge from the Arians, he came to Rome, introduced the custom to the Western Church.

St. Ambrose worked vigorously in this direction, not only in his own diocese, but in neighboring provinces, and even in Africa. Early in his episcopate he addressed his flock on the subject, and at the request of his sister, Marcellina, gathered up his teaching in the following three books.

In the first book he treats of the dignity of Virginity, and states his reason for writing. As he commences his addresses on the anniversary of the martyrdom of St. Agnes, he takes her story as the subject of the earlier part of the treatise, and shows how, amongst the Jews, and even amongst the heathen, the grace of virginity was shadowed forth, and eventually proclaimed by the corning of our Lord. He then warns parents, especially widows, not to prevent their daughters from hearing addresses on this subject, and touches on the number of those who came even from great distances to receive the veil at Milan.

In the second book, speaking of the character and manner of life of virgins, he does this, as he says, by adducing examples and instances, preferably to laying down a code of rules. He speaks of Thecla, patron saint of Milan, a disciple of St. Paul, and of other virgins.

In the third book he goes through a summary of the address given by Pope Liberius, when Marcellina received the veil at his hands, before a large congregation. Some cautions are introduced by St. Ambrose against excessive austerity, and instead of some outward acts, prayer and the practice of interior virtues are recommended. The subject of certain virgins who had committed suicide rather than lose their chastity is dwelt upon in answer to a question of Marcellina.

The writer himself states that this treatise was composed in the third year of his episcopate, A.D. 377, and it is quoted with approval by St. Jerome, *Ep.* XXII. 22 and XLVIII. 14 [Vol. VI., pp. 31 and 75, of this series, and St. Augustine, *de doct. Christ.* IV. 48, 50.

THE BOOKS CONCERNING VIRGINS
To Marcellina, His Sister.

BOOK I.

CHAPTER I.

St. Ambrose, reflecting upon the account he will have to give of his talents, determines to write, and consoles himself with certain examples of God's mercy. Then recognizing his own deficiencies desires that he may be dealt with like the fig-tree in the Gospel, and expresses a hope that words will not fail him in his endeavor to preach Christ.

1. IF, according to the decree of heavenly truth, we have to give account of every idle word which we have spoken, and if every servant will incur no small blame when his lord returns, who, either like a timid money-lender or covetous owner, has hidden in the earth the talents of spiritual grace which were entrusted to him in order that they might be multiplied by increasing interest, I, who, although possessed of but moderate ability, yet have a great necessity laid on me of making increase of the sayings of God entrusted to me, must rightly fear lest an account of the profit of my words be demanded of me, especially seeing that the Lord exacts of us effort, not profit. Wherefore I determined to write something, since, too, my words are listened to with greater risk to modesty than when they are written, for a book has no feeling of modesty.

2. And so distrusting indeed my own ability, but encouraged by the instances of divine mercy, I venture to

compose an address, for when God willed even the ass spoke. And I will open my mouth long dumb, that the angel may assist me also, engaged in the burdens of this world, for He can do away with the hindrances of unskillfulness, Who in the ass did away those of nature. In the ark of the Old Testament the priest's rod budded;[3163] with God it is easy that in Holy Church a flower should spring from our knots also. And why should we despair that God should speak in men, Who spoke in the thorn bush? God did not despise the bush, and would He might give light also to my thorns. Perhaps some may wonder that there is some light even in our thorns; some our thorns will not burn; there will be some whose shoes shall be put off their feet at the sound of my voice, that the steps of the mind may be freed from bodily hindrances.

3. But these things are gained by holy men. Would that Jesus would cast a glance upon me still lying under that barren fig-tree, and that my fig-tree might also after three years bear fruit. But whence should sinners have so great hope? Would that at least that Gospel dresser of the vineyard, perhaps already bidden to cut down my fig-tree, would let it alone this year also, until he dig about it and dung it, that he may perchance lift the helpless out of the dust, and lift the poor out of the mire. Blessed are they who bind their horses under the vine and olive, consecrating the course of their labors to light and joy: the fig-tree, that is, the tempting attraction of the pleasures of the world, still overshadows me, low in height, brittle for working, soft for use, and barren of fruit.

4. And perhaps someone may wonder why I, who cannot speak, venture to write. And yet if we consider what we

read in the writings of the Gospel, and the deeds of the priests, and the holy prophet Zacharias is taken as an instance, he will find that there is something which the voice cannot explain, but the pen can write. And if the name John restored speech to his father, I, too, ought not to despair that although dumb I may yet receive speech, if I speak of Christ, of Whom, according to the prophet's word: "Who shall declare the generation?" And so as a servant I will announce the family of the Lord, for the Lord has consecrated to Himself a family even in this body of humanity replete with frailty.

CHAPTER II.

This treatise has a favorable beginning, since it is the birthday of the holy Virgin Agnes, of whose name, modesty, and martyrdom St. Ambrose speaks in commendation, but more especially of her age, seeing that she, being but twelve years old, was superior to terrors, promises, tortures, and death itself, with a courage wholly worthy of a man.

5. AND my task begins favorably, that since to-day is the birthday of a virgin, I have to speak of virgins, and the treatise has its beginning from this discourse. It is the birthday of a martyr, let us offer the victim. It is the birthday of St. Agnes, let men admire, let children take courage, let the married be astounded, let the unmarried take an example. But what can I say worthy of her whose very name was not devoid of bright praise? In devotion beyond her age, in virtue above nature, she seems to me to have borne not so much a human name, as a token of martyrdom, whereby she showed what she was to be.

6. But I have that which may assist me. The name of virgin is a title of modesty. I will call upon the martyr, I will proclaim the virgin. That panegyric is long enough which needs no elaboration, but is within our grasp. Let then labor cease, eloquence be silent. One word is praise enough. This word old men and young and boys chant. No one is more praiseworthy than he who can be praised by all. There are as many heralds as there are men, who when they speak proclaim the martyr.

7. She is said to have suffered martyrdom when twelve years old. The more hateful was the cruelty, which spared not so tender an age, the greater in truth was the power of faith which found evidence even in that age. Was there

room for a wound in that small body? And she who had no room for the blow of the steel had that wherewith to conquer the steel. But maidens of that age are unable to bear even the angry looks of parents, and are wont to cry at the pricks of a needle as though they were wounds. She was fearless under the cruel hands of the executioners, she was unmoved by the heavy weight of the creaking chains, offering her whole body to the sword of the raging soldier, as yet ignorant of death, but ready for it. Or if she were unwillingly hurried to the altars, she was ready to stretch forth her hands to Christ at the sacrificial fires, and at the sacrilegious altars themselves, to make the sign of the Lord the Conqueror, or again to place her neck and both her hands in the iron bands, but no band could enclose such slender limbs.

8. A new kind of martyrdom! Not yet of fit age for punishment but already ripe for victory, difficult to contend with but easy to be crowned, she filled the office of teaching valor while having the disadvantage of youth. She would not as a bride so hasten to the couch, as being a virgin she joyfully went to the place of punishment with hurrying step, her head not adorned with plaited hair, but with Christ. All wept, she alone was without a tear. All wondered that she was so readily prodigal of her life, which she had not yet enjoyed, and now gave up as though she had gone through it. Everyone was astounded that there was now one to bear witness to the Godhead, who as yet could not, because of her age, dispose of herself. And she brought it to pass that she should be believed concerning God, whose evidence concerning man would not be accepted. For that which is beyond nature is from the Author of nature.

9. What threats the executioner used to make her fear him, what allurements to persuade her, how many desired that she would come to them in marriage! But she answered: "It would be an injury to my spouse to look on any one as likely to please me. He who chose me first for Himself shall receive me. Why are you delaying, executioner? Let this body perish which can be loved by eyes which I would not." She stood, she prayed, she bent down her neck. You could see the executioner tremble, as though he himself had been condemned, and his right-hand shake, his face grow pale, as he feared the peril of another, while the maiden feared not for her own. You have then in one victim a twofold martyrdom, of modesty and of religion. She both remained a virgin and she obtained martyrdom.

CHAPTER III.

Virginity is praised on many grounds, but chiefly because it brought down the Word from heaven, and hence its pursuit, which existed in but few under the old covenant, has spread to countless numbers.

10. AND now the love of purity draws me on, and you, my holy sister, even though not speaking in your silent habit, to say something about virginity, lest that which is a principal virtue should seem to be passed by with only a slight reference. For virginity is not praiseworthy because it is found in martyrs, but because itself makes martyrs.

11. But who can comprehend that by human understanding which not even nature has included in her laws? Or who can explain in ordinary language that which is above the course of nature? Virginity has brought from heaven that which it may imitate on earth. And not unfittingly has she sought her manner of life from heaven, who has found for herself a Spouse in heaven. She, passing beyond the clouds, air, angels, and stars, has found the Word of God in the very bosom of the Father, and has drawn Him into herself with her whole heart. For who having found so great a Good would forsake it? For "Thy Name is as ointment poured out, therefore have the maidens loved Thee, and drawn Thee." And indeed what I have said is not my own, since they who marry not nor are given in marriage are as the angels in heaven. Let us not, then, be surprised if they are compared to the angels who are joined to the Lord of angels. Who, then, can deny that this mode of life has its source in heaven, which we don't easily find on earth, except since God came down into the members of an earthly body? Then a Virgin

conceived, and the Word became flesh that flesh might become God.

12. But someone will say: "But Elijah is seen to have had nothing to do with the embraces of bodily love." And therefore was he carried by a chariot into heaven, therefore he appeared glorified with the Lord, and therefore he is to come as the forerunner of the Lord's advent. And Miriam taking the timbrel led the dances with maidenly modesty. But consider whom she was then representing. Was she not a type of the Church, who as a virgin with unstained spirit joins together the religious gatherings of the people to sing divine songs? For we read that there were virgins appointed also in the temple at Jerusalem. But what says the Apostle? "These things happened to them in a figure, that they might be signs of what was to come." For the figure is shown in few, the life exists in many.

13. But in truth after that the Lord, coming in our flesh, joined together the Godhead and flesh without any confusion or mixture, then the practice of the life of heaven spreading throughout the whole world was implanted in human bodies. This is that which angels ministering on earth signified should come to pass, which ministry should be offered to the Lord with the service of an unstained body. This is that heavenly service which the host of rejoicing angels spoke of for the earth. We have, then, the authority of antiquity from of old, the fullness of the setting forth from Christ Himself.

CHAPTER IV.

The comeliness of virginity never existed amongst the heathen, neither with the vestal virgins, nor amongst philosophers, such as Pythagoras.

14. I CERTAINLY have not this in common with the heathen, nor in regard to it am I associated with barbarians, nor practice it with other animals, with whom, although we breathe one and the same vital air, and have a common condition of an earthly body, and from whom we differ not in the mode of generation, in this point alone we nevertheless avoid the reproach of likeness, that virginity is aimed at by the heathen, but when consecrated it is violated, it is attacked by barbarians, and is unknown to others.

15. Who will allege to me the virgins of Vesta, and the priests of Pallas? What sort of chastity is that which is not of morals, but of years, which is appointed not forever, but for a term! Such purity is all the more wanton of which the corruption is put off for a later age. They teach their virgins ought not to persevere, and are unable to do so, who have set a term to virginity. What sort of a religion is that in which modest maidens are bidden to be immodest old women? Nor is she modest who is bound by law, and she immodest who is set free by law. O the mystery! O the morals! where chastity is enforced by law and authority given for lust! And so she is not chaste, who is constrained by fear; nor honorable, who is hired for a price; nor is that modesty which, exposed to the daily importunity of lascivious eyes, is attacked by disgraceful looks. Exemptions are bestowed upon them, prices are offered them, as though to sell one's chastity were not the

greatest sign of wantonness. That which is promised for a price is given up for a price; is made over for a price; is considered to have its price. She who is wont to sell her chastity knows not how to redeem it.

16. What shall I say of the Phrygian rites, in which immodesty is the rule, and that too of the weaker sex? What of the orgies of Bacchus, where the mystery of the rites is an incentive to lust? Of what sort can the lives of priests be, then, where the adulteries of the gods are matters of religion. So then they have no sacred virgins.

17. Let us see whether perchance the precepts of philosophers have formed any, for they are wont to claim the teaching of all virtues. A certain Pythagorean virgin is spoken of in story, whom a tyrant was endeavoring to compel to reveal the secret, and lest it should be possible even in her torments for revelation to be extorted from her, she bit off her tongue and spat it in the tyrant's face, that he who would not make an end of questioning might not have ought to question.

18. But that same virgin, so constant in mind, was overcome by lust, though she could not be overcome by torments. And so she who could keep the secret of her mind could not conceal the shame of her body. She overcame nature, but observed not discipline. How she would desire that her speech had existed as a defense of her chastity! So she was not unconquered on every side, for although the tyrant could not find out that which he sought, yet he did find what he sought not.

19. How much stronger are our virgins, who overcome even those powers which they do not see; whose victory is not only over flesh and blood, but also over the prince of this world, and ruler of this age! In age, Agnes indeed was less, but in virtue greater, triumphing over more, more constant in her confidence; she did not destroy her tongue through fear, but kept it for a trophy. For there was nothing in her which she feared to betray, since that which she acknowledged was holy, not sinful. And so the former merely concealed her secret, the latter bore witness to the Lord, and confessed Him in her body, Whom her age did not yet suffer to confess.

CHAPTER V.

Heaven is the home of virginity, and the Son of God its Author, Who though He was a Virgin before the Virgin, yet being of the Virgin took the Virgin Church as His bride. Of her we have all been born. Some of her gifts are enumerated. Her daughters have a special excellence in that virginity is not a matter of precept, and that it is a most powerful help in the pursuit of piety.

20. It is the custom in encomiums to speak of country and parentage of the subject, that the greatness of the offspring may be enhanced by mention of the father. Now I, who have not undertaken to praise but to set forth virginity, yet think it to the purpose to make known its country and its parent. First, let us settle where is its country. Now, if one's country be there where is the home of one's birth, without doubt heaven is the native country of chastity. And so she is a stranger here, but a denizen there.

21. And what is virginal chastity but purity free from stain? And whom can we judge to be its author but the immaculate Son of God, Whose flesh saw no corruption, Whose Godhead experienced no infection? Consider, then, how great are the merits of virginity. Christ was before the Virgin; Christ was of the Virgin. Begotten indeed of the Father before the ages, but born of the Virgin for the ages. The former was of His own nature; the latter is for our benefit. The former always was, the latter He willed.

22. Consider, too, another merit of virginity. Christ is the spouse of the Virgin, and if one may so say of virginal chastity, for virginity is of Christ, not Christ of virginity. He is, then, the Virgin Who was espoused, the Virgin

Who bare us, Who fed us with her own milk, of whom we read: "How great things hath the virgin of Jerusalem done! The teats shall not fail from the rock, nor snow from Lebanon, nor the water which is borne by the strong wind." Who is this virgin that is watered with the streams of the Trinity, from whose rock waters flow, whose teats fail not, and whose honey is poured forth? Now, according to the Apostle, the rock is Christ. Therefore, from Christ the teats fail not, nor brightness from God, nor the river from the Spirit. This is the Trinity which waters their Church, the Father, Christ, and the Spirit.

23. But let us now come down from the mother to the daughters. "Concerning virgins," says the Apostle, "I have no commandment of the Lord." If the teacher of the Gentiles had none, who could have one? And in truth he had no commandment, but he had an example. For virginity cannot be commanded, but must be wished for, for things which are above us are matters for prayer rather than under mastery. "But I would have you," he says, "be without carefulness. For he who is without a wife is careful for the things which are the Lord's, how he may please God....And the virgin taketh thought for the things of the Lord, that she may be holy in body and in spirit. For she that is married taketh thought for the things of the world, how she may please her husband."

CHAPTER VI.

St. Ambrose explains that he is not speaking against marriage, and proceeds to compare the advantages and disadvantages of the single and married state.

24. I AM not indeed discouraging marriage, but am enlarging upon the benefits of virginity. "He who is weak," says the Apostle, "eats herbs." I consider one thing necessary, I admire another. "Art thou bound to a wife? Seek not to be loosed. Art thou free from a wife? Seek not a wife." This is the command to those who are. But what does he say concerning virgins? "He who giveth his virgin in marriage doeth well, and he who giveth her not doeth better." The one sins not if she marries, the other, if she marries not, it is for eternity. In the former is the remedy for weakness, in the latter the glory of chastity. The former is not reproved; the latter is praised.

25. Let us compare, if it pleases you, the advantages of married women with that which awaits virgins. Though the noble woman boasts of her abundant offspring, yet the more she bears the more she endures. Let her count up the comforts of her children, but let her likewise count up the troubles. She marries and weeps. How many vows does she make with tears. She conceives, and her fruitfulness brings her trouble before offspring. She brings forth and is ill. How sweet a pledge which begins with danger and ends in danger, which will cause pain before pleasure! It is purchased by perils, and is not possessed at her own will.

26. Why speak of the troubles of nursing, training, and marrying? These are the miseries of those who are

fortunate. A mother has heirs, but it increases her sorrows. For we must not speak of adversity, lest the minds of the holiest parents tremble. Consider, my sister, how hard it must be to bear what one must not speak of. And this is in this present age. But the days shall come when they shall say: "Blessed are the barren, and the wombs that never bare." For the daughters of this age are conceived, and conceive; but the daughter of the kingdom refrains from wedded pleasure, and the pleasure of the flesh, that she may be holy in body and in spirit.

27. Why should I further speak of the painful ministrations and services due to their husbands from wives, to whom before slaves God gave the command to serve? And I mention these things that they may comply more willingly, whose reward, if approved, is love; if not approved, punishment for the fault.

28. And in this position spring up those incentives to vice, in that they paint their faces with various colors, fearing not to please their husbands; and from staining their faces, come to think of staining their chastity. What madness is here, to change the fashion of nature and seek a painting, and while fearing a husband's judgment to give up their own. For she is the first to speak against herself who wishes to change that which is natural to her. So, while studying to please others, she displeases herself. What truer witness to thy unsightliness do we require, O woman, than thyself who are afraid to be seen? If thou art beautiful, why hide thou thyself? If unsightly, why dost thou falsely pretend to beauty, so as to have neither the satisfaction of thy own conscience, nor of the error of another? For he loves another, thou desires to please

another. And art thou angry if he love another, who is taught to do so in thy own person? Thou art an evil teacher of thy own injury.

29. And next, what expense is necessary that even a beautiful wife may not fail to please? Costly necklaces on the one hand hang on her neck, on the other a robe woven with gold is dragged along the ground. Is this display purchased, or is it a real possession? And what varied enticements of perfumes are made use of! The ears are weighed down with gems, a different color from nature is dropped into the eyes. What is there left which is her own, when so much is changed? The married woman loves her own perceptions, and does she think that this is to live?

30. But you, O happy virgins, who know not such torments, rather than ornaments, whose holy modesty, beaming in your bashful cheeks, and sweet chastity are a beauty, ye do not, intent upon the eyes of men, consider as merits what is gained by the errors of others. You, too, have indeed your own beauty, furnished by the comeliness of virtue, not of the body, to which age puts not an end, which death cannot take away, nor any sickness injure. Let God alone be sought as the judge of loveliness, Who loves even in less beautiful bodies the more beautiful souls. You know nothing of the burden and pain of childbearing, but more are the offspring of a pious soul, which esteems all as its children, which is rich in successors, barren of all bereavements, which knows no deaths, but has many heirs.

31. So the holy Church, ignorant of wedlock, but fertile in bearing, is in chastity a virgin, yet a mother in offspring.

She, a virgin, bears us her children, not by a human father, but by the Spirit. She bears us not with pain, but with the rejoicings of the angels. She, a virgin, feeds us, not with the milk of the body, but with that of the Apostle, wherewith he fed the tender age of the people who were still children. For what bride has more children than holy Church, who is a virgin in her sacraments and a mother to her people, whose fertility even holy Scripture attests, saying, "For many more are the children of the desolate than of her that hath a husband"? She has not a husband, but she has a Bridegroom, inasmuch as she, whether as the Church amongst nations, or as the soul in individuals, without any loss of modesty, she weds the Word of God as her eternal Spouse, free from all injury, full of reason.

CHAPTER VII.

St. Ambrose exhorts parents to train their children to virginity, and sets before them the troubles arising from their desire to have grandchildren. He says however that he does not forbid marriage, but rather defends it against heretics who oppose it. Still setting virginity before marriage, he speaks of the beauty of their spouse, and of the gifts wherewith He adorns them, and applies to these points certain verses of the Song of Songs.

32. You have heard, O parents, in what virtues and pursuits you ought to train your daughters, that you may possess those by whose merits your faults may be redeemed. The virgin is an offering for her mother, by whose daily sacrifice the divine power is appeased. A virgin is the inseparable pledge of her parents, who neither troubles them for a dowry, nor forsakes them, nor injures them in word or deed.

33. But someone perhaps wishes to have grandchildren, and to be called grandfather. In the first place, such a one gives up what is his own, while seeking what is another's, and is already losing what is certain, while hoping to gain what is uncertain; he gives away his own riches, and still more is asked for; if he does not pay the dowry, it is exacted; if he lives long, he becomes a burden. This is to buy a son-in-law, not to gain one who would sell a sight of their daughter to her parents. Was she borne so long in her mother's womb in order that she might pass under the power of another? And so the parents take the charge of setting off their virgin that she may so be the sooner removed from them.

34. Someone may say, Do you, then, discourage marriage? Nay, I encourage it, and condemn those who

are wont to discourage it, so much so, that indeed I am wont to speak of the marriages of Sarah, Rebecca, and Rachel, and other women of old time, as instances of singular virtues. For he who condemns marriage, condemns the birth of children, and condemns the fellowship of the human race, continued by a series of successive generations. For how could generation succeed generation in a continual order, unless the gift of marriage stirred up the desire of offspring? Or how could one set forth that Isaac went to the altar of God as a victim of his father's piety, or that Israel, when yet in the body, saw God, and gave a holy name to the people while speaking against that whereby they came into being? Those men, though wicked, have one point at any rate, wherein they are approved even by the wise persons, that in speaking against marriage they declare that they ought not to have been born.

35. I do not then discourage marriage, but recapitulate the advantages of holy virginity. This is the gift of few only, that is of all. And virginity itself cannot exist, unless it have some mode of coming into existence. I am comparing good things with good things, that it may be clear which is the more excellent. Nor do I allege any opinion of my own, but I repeat that which the Holy Spirit spoke by the prophet: "Blessed is the barren that is undefiled."

36. First of all, in that which those who purpose to marry desire above all things, that they may boast of the beauty of their husband, they must of necessity confess that they are inferior to virgins, to Whom alone it is suitable to say: "Thou art fairer than the children of men, grace is poured on Thy lips." Who is that Spouse? One not given to

common indulgences, not proud of possessing riches, but He Whose throne is forever and ever. The king's daughters share in His honor: "At Thy right hand stood the queen in a vesture of gold, clothed with variety of virtues. Hearken, then, O daughter, and consider, and incline thine ear, and forget thine own people and thy father's house; for the king hath desired thy beauty, for He is thy God."

37. And observe what a kingdom the Holy Spirit by the witness of the divine Scriptures has assigned to thee—gold, and beauty; gold, either because thou art the bride of the Eternal King, or because having an unconquered mind, thou art not taken captive by the allurements of pleasures, but rules over them like a queen. Gold again, because as that metal is more precious when tried by fire, so the appearance of the virginal body, consecrated to the Divine Spirit, gains an increase of its own comeliness, for who can imagine a loveliness greater than the beauty of her who is loved by the King, approved by the judge, dedicated to the Lord, consecrated to God; ever a bride, ever unmarried, so that neither does love suffer an ending, nor modesty loss.

38. This is indeed true beauty, to which nothing is wanting, which alone is worthy to hear the Lord saying: "Thou art all fair, My love, and no blemish is in thee. Come hither from Lebanon, My spouse, come hither from Lebanon. Thou shalt pass and pass through from the beginning of faith, from the top of Sanir and Hermon, from the dens of the lions, from the mountains of the leopards." By which references is set forth the perfect and irreproachable beauty of a virgin soul, consecrated to the

altars of God, not moved by perishable things amidst the haunts and dens of spiritual wild beasts, but intent, by the mysteries of God, on being found worthy of the Beloved, Whose breasts are full of joy. For "wine makes glad the heart of man."

39. "The smell of thy garments," says He, "is above all spices." And again: "And the smell of thy garments is like the smell of Lebanon." See what progress thou sets forth, O Virgin. Thy first odor is above all spices, which were used upon the burying of the Savior, and the
fragrance arises from the mortified motions of the body, and the perishing of the delights of the members. Thy second odor, like the odor of Lebanon, exhales the incorruption of the Lord's body, the flower of virginal chastity.

CHAPTER VIII.

Taking the passage concerning the honeycomb in the Song of Songs, he expounds it, comparing the sacred virgins to bees.

40. LET, then, your work be as it were a honeycomb, for virginity is fit to be compared to bees, so laborious is it, so modest, so continent. The bee feeds on dew, it knows no marriage couch, it makes honey. The virgin's dew is the divine word, for the words of God descend like the dew. The virgin's modesty is unstained nature. The virgin's produce is the fruit of the lips, without bitterness, abounding in sweetness. They work in common, and their fruit is in common.

41. How I wish you, my daughter, to be an imitator of these bees, whose food is flowers, whose offspring is collected and brought together by the mouth. Do imitate her, my daughter. Let no veil of deceit be spread over your words; let them have no covering of guile, that they may be pure, and full of gravity.

42. And let an eternal succession of merits be brought forth by your mouth. Gather not for yourself alone (for how do you know when your soul shall be required of you?), lest leaving your granaries heaped full with corn, which will be a help neither to your life nor to your merits, you be hurried thither where you cannot take your treasure with you. Be rich then, but towards the poor, that as they share in your nature they may also share your goods.

43. And I also point out to you what flower is to be culled, that one it is Who said: "I am the Flower of the

field, and the Lily of the valleys, as a lily among thorns," which is a plain declaration that virtues are surrounded by the thorns of spiritual wickedness, so that no one can gather the fruit who does not approach with caution.

CHAPTER IX.

Other passages from the Song of Songs are considered with relation to the present subject, and St. Ambrose exhorting the virgin to seek for Christ, points out where He may be found. A description of His perfections follows, and a comparison is made between virgins and the angels.

44. TAKE, then, O Virgin, the wings of the Spirit, that you may fly far above all vices, if you wish to attain to Christ: "He dwells on high, but beholds lowly things;" and His appearance is as that of a cedar of Lebanon, which has its foliage in the clouds, its roots in the earth. For its beginning is from heaven, its ending on earth, and it produces fruit very close to heaven. Search diligently for so precious a flower, if perchance you may find it in the recesses of your breast, for it is most often to be enjoyed in lowly places.

45. It loves to grow in gardens, in which Susanna, while walking, found it, and was ready to die rather than it should be violated. But what is meant by the gardens He Himself points out, saying: "A garden enclosed is My sister, My spouse, a garden enclosed, a fountain sealed;" because in gardens of this kind the water of the pure fountain shines, reflecting the features of the image of God, lest its streams mingled with mud from the wallowing places of spiritual wild beasts should be polluted. For this reason, too, that modesty of virgins fenced in by the wall of the Spirit is enclosed lest it should lie open to be plundered. And so as a garden inaccessible from without smells of the violet, is scented with the olive, and is resplendent with the rose, that religion may increase in the vine, peace in the olive, and the modesty of consecrated virginity in the rose. This is

the odor of which the patriarch Jacob smelt when he heard his father say: "See the smell of my son is as the smell of a field which is full." For although the field of the holy patriarch was full of almost all fruits, the other brought forth its crops with greater labor, the latter flowers.

46. To work, then, O Virgin, and if you wish your garden to be sweet after this sort, enclose it with the precepts of the prophets: "Set a watch before thy mouth, and a door to thy lips," that you, too, may be able to say: "As the apple-tree among the trees of the wood, so is my Beloved among the sons. In His shadow I delighted and sat down, and His fruit was sweet to my palate.

I found Him Whom my soul loved, I held Him and would not let him go. My beloved came down into His garden to eat the fruit of His trees. Come, my Beloved, let us go forth into the field. Set me as a signet upon Thine heart, and as a seal upon Thine arm. My Beloved is white and ruddy." For it is fitting, O Virgin, that you should fully know Him Whom you love, and should recognize in Him all the mystery of His Divine Nature and the Body which He has assumed. He is white fittingly, for He is the brightness of the Father; and ruddy, for He was born of a Virgin. The color of each nature shines and glows in Him. But remember that the marks of His Godhead are more ancient in Him than the mysteries of His body, for He did not take His origin from the Virgin, but, He Who already existed came into the Virgin.

47. He Who was spoiled by the soldiers, Who was wounded by the spear, that He might heal us by the blood of His sacred wounds, will assuredly answer you (for He

is meek and lowly of heart, and gentle in aspect): "Arise, O north wind, and come, O south, and blow upon My garden, that My spices may flow out." For from all parts of the world has the perfume of holy religion increased, and the limbs of the consecrated Virgin have glowed. "Thou art beautiful, O my love, as Tirzah, comely as Jerusalem." So it is not the beauty of the perishable body, which will come to an end with sickness or old age, but the reputation for good deserts, subject to no accidents and never to perish, which is the beauty of virgins.

48. And since you are worthy to be compared not now with men but with heavenly beings, whose life you are living on earth, receive from the Lord the precepts you are to observe: "Set Me as a signet upon thine heart, and as a seal upon thine arm;" that clearer proofs of your prudence and actions may be set forth, in which Christ the Figure of God may shine, Who, equaling fully the nature of the Father, has expressed the whole which He took of the Father's Godhead. Whence also the Apostle Paul says that we are sealed in the Spirit; since we have in the Son the image of the Father, and in the Spirit the seal of the Son. Let us, then, sealed by this Trinity, take more diligent heed, lest either levity of character or the deceit of any unfaithfulness unseal the pledge which we have received in our hearts.

49. But let fear secure this for the holy virgins, for whom the Church first provided such protection, who, anxious for the prosperity of her tender offspring, herself as a wall with breasts as many towers, increases her care for them, until, the fear of hostile attack being at an end, she obtains by the care of a mother's love peace for her vigorous

children. Wherefore the prophet says: "Peace be on thy virtue, and abundance in thy towers."

50. Then the Lord of peace Himself, after having embraced in His strong arms the vineyards committed to Him, and beholding their shoots putting forth buds, with glad looks, tempers the breezes to the young fruits, as Himself testifies, saying: "My vineyard is in My sight, a thousand for Solomon, and two hundred who keep the fruit thereof."

51. Above it is said: "Sixty strong men round about its offspring, armed with drawn swords, and expert in warlike discipline," here there are a thousand and two hundred. The number has increased, where the fruit has increased, for the more holy each is, the more is he guarded. So Elisha the prophet showed the hosts of angels who were present to guard him; so Joshua the son of Nun recognized the Captain of the heavenly host. They, then, who are able also to fight for us are able to guard the fruit that is in us. And for you, holy virgins, there is a special guardianship, for you who with unspotted chastity keep the couch of the Lord holy. And no wonder if the angels fight for you who war with the mode of life of angels. Virginal chastity merits their guardianship whose life it attains to.

52. Why should I continue the praise of chastity in more words? For chastity has made even angels. He who has preserved it is an angel; he who has lost it a devil. And hence has religion also gained its name. She is a virgin who is the bride of God, a harlot who makes gods for herself. What shall I say of the resurrection of which you

already hold the rewards: "For in the resurrection they will neither be given in marriage, nor marry, but shall be," He says, "as the angels in heaven." That which is promised to us is already present with you, and the object of your prayers is with you; ye are of this world, and yet not in this world. This age has held you, but has not been able to retain you.

53. But what a great thing it is that angels because of incontinence fell from heaven into this world, that virgins because of chastity passed from the world into heaven. Blessed virgins, whom the delights of the flesh do not allure, nor the defilement of pleasures cast down. Sparing food and abstinence in drink train them in ignorance of vices, seeing they keep them from knowing the causes of vices. That which causes sin has often deceived even the just. In this way the people of God after they sat down to eat and drink denied God. In this way, too, Lot knew not, and so endured his daughters' wickedness. So, too, the sons of Noah going backward covered their father's nakedness, which he who was wanton saw, he who was modest blushed at and dutifully hid, fearful of offending if he too saw it. How great is the power of wine, so that wine made him naked which the waters of the deluge could not.

CHAPTER X.

Finally, another glory of virginity is mentioned, that it is free from avarice. St. Ambrose, addressing his sister, reminds her of the great happiness of those who are free from those troubles as to luxury and vanity which come upon those who are about to marry.

WHAT then? What happiness it is that no desire of possessions inflames you! The poor man demands what you have, he does not ask for what you have not. The fruit of your labor is a treasure for the needy, and two mites, if they be all one has, are wealth on the part of the giver.

54. Listen, then, my sister, from what you escape. For it is not for me to teach nor for you to learn what you ought to guard against, for the practice of perfect virtue does not require teaching, but instructs others. You see how like she is to the litters at processions, who lays herself out to please, attracting to herself the look and gaze of all; less beautiful is she because she strives to please, for she displeases the people before she pleases her husband. But in you the rejection of all care for splendor is far more becoming, and the very fact that you do not adorn yourselves is an ornament.

55. Look at the ears pierced with wounds, and pity the neck weighed down with burdens. That the metals are different does not lighten the suffering. In one case a chain binds the neck, in another a fetter encloses the foot. It makes no difference whether the body be loaded with gold or with iron. Thus the neck is weighed down and the steps are hindered. The price makes it no better, except that you women are afraid lest that which causes you suffering be lost. What is the difference whether the sentence of another or your own condemn you? Nay, you,

even more wretched than those, are condemned by public justice, since they desire to be set free, you to be bound.

56. But how wretched a position, that she who is marriageable is in a species of sale put up as it were to auction to be bid for, so that he who offers the highest price purchases her. Slaves are sold on more tolerable conditions, for they often choose their masters; if a maiden chooses it is an offence, if not it is an insult. And she, though she be beautiful and comely, both fears and wishes to be seen; she wishes it that she may sell herself for a better price; she fears lest the fact of her being seen should itself be unbecoming. But what absurdities of wishes and fears and suspicions are there as to how the suitors will turn out, lest a poor man may beguile her, or a rich one contemn her, lest a handsome suitor mock her, lest a noble one despise her.

CHAPTER XI.

St. Ambrose answers objections made to the uselessness of his exhortations in favor of virginity, and brings forward instances of virgins especially in various places he mentions, and speaks of their zeal in the cause.

57. SOME one may say, you are always singing the praises of virgins. What shall I do who am always singing them and have no success? But this is not my fault. Then, too, virgins come from Placentia to be consecrated, or from Bononia, and Mauritania, in order to receive the veil here. You see a striking thing here. I treat the matter here, and persuade those who are elsewhere. If this be so, let me treat the subject elsewhere, that I may persuade you.

58. What is it, then, that even they who hear me not follow my teaching, and those who hear me follow me not? For I have known many virgins who had the desire, but were prevented from going forward by their mothers, and, which is more serious, mothers who were widows, to whom I will now address myself. For if your daughters desired to love a man, they could, by law, choose whom they would. Are they, then, who are allowed to choose a man not allowed to choose God?

59. Behold how sweet is the fruit of modesty, which has sprung up even in the affections of barbarians. Virgins coming from the most distant on this and that side of Mauritania desire to be consecrated here; and though all the families be in bonds, yet modesty cannot be bound. She who mourns over the hardship of slavery avows an eternal kingdom.

60. And what shall I say of the virgins of Bononia, a fertile band of chastity, who, forsaking worldly delights, inhabit the sanctuary of virginity? Not being of the sex which lives in common, attaining in their common chastity to the number of twenty, and fruit to a hundredfold, leaving their parents' dwelling they press into the houses of Christ, as soldiers of unwearied chastity; at one time singing spiritual songs, they provide their sustenance by labor, and seek with their hands supplies for their liberality.

61. But if the attraction of searching for virgins has grown strong (for they beyond others follow up the search and watch for purity), they follow up their hidden prey with the greatest perseverance to its very chambers; or, if the flight of any one shall have seemed more free, one may see them rise on the wing, hear the rustling of their feathers, and the bursting of applause; so as to surround the one on wing with a chaste band of modesty, until rejoicing in that fair companionship, forgetful of her father's house, she enters the regions of modesty and the fenced-in home of chastity.

CHAPTER XII.

It is very desirable that parents should encourage the desire for the virgin life, but more praiseworthy when the love of God draws a maiden even against their will. The violence of parents and the loss of property are not to be feared, and an instance of this is related by St. Ambrose.

62. It is a good thing, then, that the zeal of parents, like favoring gales, should aid a virgin; but it is more glorious if the fire of tender age even without the incitement of those older of its own self burst forth into the flame of chastity. Parents will refuse a dowry, but you have a wealthy Spouse, satisfied with Whose treasures you will not miss the revenues of a father's inheritance.
How much is poverty to chastity superior to bridal gifts!

63. And yet of whom have you heard as ever, because of her desire for chastity, having been deprived of her lawful inheritance? Parents speak against her, but are willing to be overcome. They resist at first because they are afraid to believe; they often are angry that one may learn to overcome; they threaten to disinherit to try whether one is able not to fear temporal loss; they caress with exquisite allurements to see if one cannot be softened by the inducement of various pleasures. You are being exercised, O virgin, whilst you are being urged. And the anxious entreaties of your parents are your first battles. Conquer your affection first, O maiden. If you conquer your home, you conquer the world.

64. But suppose that the loss of your patrimony awaits you; are not the future realms of heaven a compensation for perishable and frail possessions? For if we believe the

heavenly message, "there is no one who has forsaken house, or parents, or brethren, or wife, or children, for the kingdom of God's sake, who shall not receive sevenfold more in this present time, and in the world to come shall have everlasting life." Entrust your faith to God, who entrust your money to man; lend to Christ. The faithful keeper of the deposit of your hope pays the talent of your faith with manifold interest. The Truth does not deceive, Justice does not circumvent, Virtue does not deceive. But if you believe not God's word, at least believe instances.

65. Within my memory a girl once noble in the world, now more noble in the sight of God, being urged to a marriage by her parents and kinsfolk, took refuge at the holy altar. Whither could a virgin better flee, than thither where the Virgin Sacrifice is offered? Nor was even that the limit of her boldness. She, the oblation of modesty, the victim of chastity, was standing at the altar of
God, now placing upon her head the right hand of the priest, asking his prayers, and now impatient at the righteous delay, placing the top of her head under the altar. "Can any better veil," she said, "cover me better than the altar which consecrates the veils themselves? Such a bridal veil is most suitable on which Christ, the Head of all, is daily consecrated. What are you doing, my kinsfolk? Why do you still trouble my mind with seeking marriage? I have long since provided for that. Do you offer me a bridegroom? I have found a better. Make the most you can of my wealth, boast of his nobility, extol his power, I have Him with Whom no one can compare himself, rich in the world, powerful in empire, noble in heaven. If you have such a one, I do not reject the choice;

if you do not find such, you do me not a kindness, my relatives, but an injury."

66. When the others were silent, one burst forth somewhat roughly: "If," he said, "your father were alive, would he suffer you to remain unmarried?" Then she replied with more religion and more restrained piety: "And perchance he is gone that no one may be able to hinder me." Which answer concerning her father, but warning as to himself, he made good by his own speedy death. So the others, each of them, fearing the same for himself, began to assist and not to hinder her as before, and her virginity involved not the loss of the property due to her, but also received the reward of her integrity. You see, maidens, the reward of devotion, and do you, parents, be warned by the example of transgression.

BOOK II.

CHAPTER I.

In this book St. Ambrose purposes to treat of the training of virgins, using examples rather than precepts, and explains why he does so in writing rather than by word of mouth.

1. IN the former book I wished (though I was not able) to set forth how great is the gift of virginity, that the grace of the heavenly gift might of itself invite the reader. In the second book it is fitting that the virgin should be instructed and, as it were, be educated by the teaching of suitable precepts.

2. But, inasmuch as I am feeble in advising and unequal to teaching (for he who teaches ought to excel him who is taught), lest I should seem to have abandoned the task I have undertaken, or to have taken too much upon myself, I thought it better to instruct by examples than by precepts; for more progress may be made by means of an example, inasmuch as that which has been already done is considered to be not difficult, and that which has been tried to be expedient, and that which has been transmitted in succession to us by a kind of hereditary practice of ancestral virtue to be binding in religion.

3. But if any one rebukes me for presumption, let him rather rebuke me for zeal, because I thought that I ought not to refuse even this to the virgins who asked it of me. For I preferred rather to run the risk of periling my own modesty, than not to fulfil the wish of those whose pursuits even our God favors with kindly approbation.

4. Nor can the mark of presumption be set on my task, since, when they had those from whom they could learn, they sought my good-will rather than my teaching, and my zeal may be excused, since when they had the guidance of a martyr for the observance of discipline, I did not think it superfluous if I could turn the persuasion of my discourse into an allurement to profession. He who teaches with facility restrains fault with severity; I, who cannot teach, entice.

5. And because many who were absent desired to have the use of my discourse, I compiled this book, in order that holding in their hands the substance of what my voice had uttered to them, they might not think that he whom they were holding failed them. But let us go on with our plan.

CHAPTER II.

The life of Mary is set before virgins as an example, and her many virtues are dwelt upon, her chastity, humility, hard life, love of retirement, and the like; then her kindness to others, her zeal in learning, and love of frequenting the temple. St. Ambrose then sets forth how she, adorned with all these virtues, will come to meet the numberless bands of virgins and lead them with great triumph to the bridal chamber of the Spouse.

6. LET, then, the life of Mary be as it were virginity itself, set forth in a likeness, from which, as from a mirror, the appearance of chastity and the form of virtue is reflected. From this you may take your pattern of life, showing, as an example, the clear rules of virtue: what you have to correct, to effect, and to hold fast.

7. The first thing which kindles ardor in learning is the greatness of the teacher. What is greater than the Mother of God? What more glorious than she whom Glory Itself chose? What more chaste than she who bore a body without contact with another body? For why should I speak of her other virtues? She was a virgin not only in body but also in mind, who stained the sincerity of its disposition by no guile, who was humble in heart, grave in speech, prudent in mind, sparing of words, studious in reading, resting her hope not on uncertain riches, but on the prayer of the poor, intent on work, modest in discourse; wont to seek not man but God as the judge of her thoughts, to injure no one, to have goodwill towards all, to rise up before her elders, not to envy her equals, to avoid boastfulness, to follow reason, to love virtue. When did she pain her parents even by a look? When did she disagree with her neighbors? When did she despise the lowly? When did she avoid the needy? Being wont only

to go to such gatherings of men as mercy would not blush at, nor modesty pass by. There was nothing gloomy in her eyes, nothing forward in her words, nothing unseemly in her acts, there was not a silly movement, nor unrestrained step, nor was her voice petulant, that the very appearance of her outward being might be the image of her soul, the representation of what is approved. For a well-ordered house ought to be recognized on the very threshold, and should show at the very first entrance that no darkness is hidden within, as our soul hindered by no restraints of the body may shine abroad like a lamp placed within.

8. Why should I detail her sparseness of food, her abundance of services—the one abounding beyond nature, the other almost insufficient for nature? And there were no seasons of slackness, but days of fasting, one upon the other. And if ever the desire for refreshment came, her food was generally what came to hand, taken to keep off death, not to minister to comfort. Necessity before inclination caused her to sleep, and yet when her body was sleeping her soul was awake, and often in sleep either went again through what had been read, or went on with what had been interrupted by sleep, or carried out what had been designed, or foresaw what was to be carried out.

9. She was unaccustomed to go from home, except for divine service, and this with parents or kinsfolk. Busy in private at home, accompanied by others abroad, yet with no better guardian than herself, as she, inspiring respect by her gait and address, progressed not so much by the motion of her feet as by step upon step of virtue. But though the Virgin had other persons who were protectors

of her body, she alone guarded her character; she can learn many points if she be her own teacher, who possesses the perfection of all virtues, for whatever she did is a lesson. Mary attended to everything as though she were warned by many, and fulfilled every obligation of virtue as though she were teaching rather than learning.

10. Such has the Evangelist shown her, such did the angel find her, such did the Holy Spirit choose her. Why delay about details? How her parents loved her, strangers praised her, how worthy she was that the Son of God should be born of her. She, when the angel entered, was found at home in privacy, without a companion, that no one might interrupt her attention or disturb her; and she did not desire any women as companions, who had the companionship of good thoughts. Moreover, she seemed to herself to be less alone when she was alone. For how should she be alone, who had with her so many books, so many archangels, so many prophets?

11. And so, too, when Gabriel visited her, did he find her, and Mary trembled, being disturbed, as though at the form of a man, but on hearing his name recognized him as one not unknown to her. And so she was a stranger as to men, but not as to the angel; that we might know that her ears were modest and her eyes bashful. Then when saluted she kept silence, and when addressed she answered, and she whose feelings were first troubled afterwards promised obedience.

12. And holy Scripture points out how modest she was towards her neighbors. For she became more humble when she knew herself to be chosen of God, and went

forthwith to her kinswoman in the hill country, not in order to gain belief by anything external, for she had believed the word of God. "Blessed," she said, "art thou who didst believe." And she abode with her three months. Now in such an interval of time it is not that faith is being sought for, but kindness which is being shown. And this was after that the child, leaping in his mother's womb, had saluted the mother of the Lord, attaining to reason before birth.

13. And then, in the many subsequent wonders, when the barren bore a son, the virgin conceived, the dumb spoke, the wise men worshipped, Simeon waited, the stars gave notice. Mary, who was moved by the angel's entrance, was unmoved by the miracles. "Mary," it is said, "kept all these things in her heart." Though she was the mother of the Lord, yet she desired to learn the precepts of the Lord, and she who brought forth God, yet desired to know God.

14. And then, how she also went every year to Jerusalem at the solemn day of the Passover, and went with Joseph. Everywhere is modesty the companion of her singular virtues in the Virgin. This, without which virginity cannot exist, must be the inseparable companion of virginity. And so Mary did not go even to the temple without the guardianship of her modesty.

15. This is the likeness of virginity. For Mary was such that her example alone is a lesson for all. If, then, the author displeases us not, let us make trial of the production, that whoever desires its reward for herself may imitate the pattern. How many kinds of virtues shine forth in one Virgin! The secret of modesty, the banner of

faith, the service of devotion, the Virgin within the house, the companion for the ministry, the mother at the temple.

16. Oh! how many virgins shall she meet, how many shall she embrace and bring to the Lord, and say: "She has been faithful to her espousal, to my Son; she has kept her bridal couch with spotless modesty." How shall the Lord Himself commend them to His Father, repeating again those words of His: "Holy Father, these are they whom I have kept for Thee, on whom the Son of Man leant His head and rested; I ask that where I am there they may be with Me." And if they ought to benefit not themselves only, who lived not for themselves alone, one virgin may redeem her parents, another her brothers. "Holy Father, the world hath not known Me, but these have known Me, and have willed not to know the world."

17. What a procession shall that be, what joy of applauding angels when she is found worthy of dwelling in heaven who lived on earth a heavenly life! Then too Mary, taking her timbrel, shall stir up the choirs of virgins, singing to the Lord because they have passed through the sea of this world without suffering from the waves of this world. Then each shall rejoice, saying: "I will go to the altar of God; to God Who makes my youth glad;" and, "I will offer unto God thanksgiving, and pay my vows unto the Most High."

18. Nor would I hesitate to admit you to the altars of God, whose souls I would without hesitation call altars, on which Christ is daily offered for the redemption of the body. For if the virgin's body be a temple of God, what is her soul, which, the ashes, as it were, of the body being shaken off, once more uncovered by the hand of the

Eternal Priest, exhales the vapor of the divine fire. Blessed virgins, who emit a fragrance through divine grace as gardens do through flowers, temples through religion, altars through the priest.

CHAPTER III.

St. Ambrose having set forth the Virgin Mary as a pattern for life, adduces Thecla as a model for learning how to die. Thecla suffered not from the beasts to whom she was condemned, but on the contrary received from them signs of reverence. He then proceeds to introduce a more recent example.

19. LET, then, holy Mary instruct you in the discipline of life, and Thecla teach you how to be offered, for she, avoiding nuptial intercourse, and condemned through her husband's rage, changed even the disposition of wild beasts by their reverence for virginity. For being made ready for the wild beasts, when avoiding the gaze of men, she offered her vital parts to a fierce lion, caused those who had turned away their immodest looks to turn them back modestly.

20. The beast was to be seen lying on the ground, licking her feet, showing without a sound that it could not injure the sacred body of the virgin. So the beast reverenced his prey, and forgetful of his own nature, put on that nature which men had lost. One could see, as it were, by some transfusion of nature, men clothed with savageness, goading the beast to cruelty, and the beast kissing the feet of the virgin, teaching them what was due from men. Virginity has in itself so much that is admirable, that even lions admire it. Food did not induce them though kept without their meal; no impulse hurried them on when excited; anger did not exasperate them when stirred up, nor did their habits lead them blindly as they were wont, nor their own natural disposition possess them with fierceness. They set an example of piety when reverencing the martyr; and gave a lesson in favor of chastity when they did nothing but kiss the virgin's feet,

with their eyes turned to the ground, as though through modesty, fearing that any male, even a beast, should see the virgin naked.

21. Someone will say: "Why have you brought forward the example of Mary, as if anyone could be found to imitate the Lord's mother? And why that of Thecla, whom the Apostle of the Gentiles trained? Give us a teacher of our own sort if you wish for disciples." I will, therefore, set before you a recent example of this sort, that you may understand that the Apostle is the teacher, not of one only, but of all.

CHAPTER IV.

A virgin at Antioch, having refused to sacrifice to idols, was condemned to a house of ill-fame, whence she escaped unharmed, having changed clothes with a Christian soldier. Then when he was condemned for this, she returned and the two contended for the prize of martyrdom, which was at last given to each.

22. THERE was lately at Antioch a virgin who avoided being seen in public, but the more she shrank from men's eyes, the more they longed for her. For beauty which is heard of but not seen is more desired, there being two incentives to passion, love and knowledge—so long as nothing is met with which pleases less; and that which pleases is thought to be of more worth, because the eye is not in this case the judge by investigation, but the mind inflamed with love is full of longing. And so the holy virgin, lest their passions should be longer fed by the desire of gaining her, professed her intention of preserving her chastity, and so quenched the fires of those wicked men, that she was no longer loved, but informed against.

23. So a persecution arose. The maiden, not knowing how to escape, and afraid lest she might fall into the hands of those who were plotting against her chastity, prepared her soul for heroic virtue, being so religious as not to fear death, so chaste as to expect it. The day of her crown arrived. The expectation of all was at its height. The maiden is brought forward, and makes her twofold profession, of religion and of chastity. But when they saw the constancy of her profession, her fear for her modesty, her readiness for tortures, and her blushes at being looked on, they began to consider how they might overcome her religion by setting chastity before her, so that, having

deprived her of that which was the greatest, they might also deprive her of that which they had left. So the sentence was that she should either sacrifice, or be sent to a house of ill-fame. After what manner do they worship their gods who thus avenge them, or how do they live themselves who give sentence after this fashion?

24. And the virgin, not hesitating about her religion, but fearful as to her chastity, began to reflect, What am I to do? Each crown, that of martyrdom and that of virginity, is grudged me to-day. But the name of virgin is not acknowledged where the Author of virginity is denied. How can one be a virgin who cherishes a harlot? How can one be a virgin who loves adulterers? How a virgin if she seeks for a lover? It is preferable to have a virgin mind than a virgin body. Each is good if each be possible; if it be not possible, let me be chaste, not to man but to God. Rahab, too, was a harlot, but after she believed in God, she found salvation. And Judith adorned herself that she might please an adulterer, but because she did this for religion and not for love, no one considered her an adulteress. This instance turned out well. For if she who entrusted herself to religion both preserved her chastity and her country, perhaps I, by preserving my religion, shall also preserve my chastity. But if Judith had preferred her chastity to her religion, when her country had been lost, she would also have lost her chastity.

25. And so, instructed by such examples, and at the same time bearing in mind the words of the Lord, where He says: "Whosoever shall lose his life for My sake, shall find it," she wept, and was silent, that the adulterer might not even hear her speaking, and she did not choose the

wrong done to her modesty, but rejected wrong done to Christ. Consider whether it was possible for her to suffer her body to be unchaste, who guarded even her speech.

26. For some time my words have been becoming bashful, and fear to laud on or describe the wicked series of what was done. Close your ears, ye virgins! The Virgin of God is taken to a house of shame. But now unclose your ears, ye virgins. The Virgin of Christ can be exposed to shame, but cannot be contaminated. Everywhere she is the Virgin of God, and the Temple of God, and houses of ill-fame cannot injure chastity, but chastity does away with the ill-fame of the place.

27. A great rush of wanton men is made to the place. Listen, ye holy virgins, to the miracles of the martyr, forget the name of the place. The door is shut within, the hawks cry without; some are contending who shall first attack the prey. But she, with her hands raised to heaven, as though she had come to a house of prayer, not to a resort of lust, says: "O Christ, Who didst tame the fierce lions for the virgin Daniel, Thou canst also tame the fierce minds of men. Fire became as dew to the Hebrew children, the water stood up for the Jews, of Thy mercy, not of its own nature. Susanna knelt down for punishment and triumphed over her adulterous accusers, the right hand withered which violated the gifts of Thy temple; and now thy temple itself is violated; suffer not sacrilegious incest, Thou Who didst not suffer theft. Let Thy Name be now again glorified in that I who came here for shame, may go away a virgin!"

28. Scarcely had she finished her prayer, when, lo! a man with the aspect of a terrible warrior burst in. How the virgin trembled before him to whom the trembling people gave way. But she did not forget what she had read. "Daniel," said she, "had gone to see the punishment of Susanna, and alone pronounced her guiltless, whom the people had condemned. A sheep may be hidden in the shape of this wolf. Christ has His soldiers also, Who is Master of legions. Or, perchance, an executioner has come in. Fear not, my soul, such a one makes martyrs. O Virgin! thy faith has saved thee."

29. And the soldier said to her: "Fear not, sister, I pray you. I, a brother, am come hither to save life, not to destroy it. Save me, that you yourself may be saved. I came in like an adulterer, to go forth, if you will, as a martyr. Let us change our attire, mine will fit you, and yours will fit me, and each for Christ. Your robe will make me a true soldier, mine will make you a virgin. You will be clothed well, I shall be unclothed even better that the persecutor may recognize me. Take the garment which will conceal the woman, give me that which shall consecrate me a martyr. Put on the cloak which will hide the limbs of a virgin, but preserve her modesty. Take the cap which will cover your hair and conceal your countenance. They who have entered houses of ill-fame are wont to blush. When you have gone forth, take care not to look back, remembering Lot's wife, who lost her very nature because she looked back at what was unchaste, though with chaste eyes. And be not afraid lest any part of the sacrifice fail. I will offer the victim to God for you, do you offer the soldier to Christ for me. You have served the good service of chastity, the wages of

which are everlasting life; you have the breastplate of righteousness, which protects the body with spiritual armor, the shield of faith with which to ward off wounds, and the helmet of salvation, for there is the defense of our salvation where Christ is, since the man is the head of the woman. and Christ of the virgin."

30. Whilst saying this he put off his cloak. This garment has been up to this time suspected of being that of a persecutor and adulterer. The virgin offered her neck, the soldier his cloak. What a spectacle that was, what a manifestation of grace when they were contending for martyrdom in a house of ill-fame! Let the characters be also considered, a soldier and a virgin, that is, persons unlike in natural disposition, but alike by the mercy of God, that the saying might be fulfilled: "Then the wolves and the lambs shall feed together." Behold the lamb and the wolf not only feed together but are also offered together. Why should I say more? Having changed her garment, the maiden flies from the snare, not now with wings of her own, seeing she was born on spiritual wings, and (a sight which the ages had never seen) she leaves the house of ill-fame a virgin, but a virgin of Christ.

31. But they who were looking with their eyes, yet saw not, raged like robbers for prey, or wolves for a lamb. One who was more shameless went in. But when he took in the state of the matter with his eyes, he said, What is this? A maiden entered, now a man is to be seen here. This is not the old fable of a hind instead of a maiden, but in truth a virgin become a soldier. I had heard but believed not that Christ changed water into wine; now He has begun also to change the sexes. Let us depart hence whilst we

still are what we were. Am I too changed who see things differently from what I believe them to be? I came to a house of ill-fame, and see a surety. And yet I go forth changed, for I shall go out chaste who came in unchaste.

32. When the affair was known, because a crown was due to such a conqueror, he was condemned for the virgin who was seized for the virgin, and so not only a virgin but a martyr came forth from the house of ill-fame. It is reported that the maiden ran to the place of punishment, and that they both contended for death. He said: "I am condemned to death, the sentence let you go free when it retained me." And she replied: "I did not choose you as my surety on pain of death, but as a guarantee for my chastity. If chastity be attacked, my sex remains; if blood is sought, I desire none to give bail for me, I have the means to pay. The sentence was pronounced on me, which was pronounced for me. Undoubtedly, if I had offered you as security for my debt, and in my absence the judge had assigned your property to the creditor, you would share the sentence with me, and I should pay your obligations with my patrimony. Were I to refuse, who would not judge me worthy of a shameful death? How much more am I bound where there is a question of death? Let me die innocent, that I may not die guilty. In this matter there is no middle course; today I shall either be guilty of your blood or a martyr in my own. If I came back quickly, who dares to shut me out? If I delayed, who dares acquit me? I owe a greater debt to the laws who am guilty not only of my own flight, but also of the death of another. My limbs are equal to death, which were not equal to dishonor. A virgin can accept a wound who could not accept contumely. I avoided disgrace, not

martyrdom. I gave up my robe to you; I did not alter my profession. And if you deprive me of death, you will not have rescued but circumvented me. Beware, pray, of resisting, beware of venturing to contend with me. Take not away the kindness you have conferred on me. In denying me the execution of this sentence, you are setting up again the former one. For the sentence is changed for a former one. If the latter binds me not, the former one does. We can each satisfy the sentence if you suffer me to be slain first. From you they can exact no other penalty, but her chastity is in danger with a virgin. And so you will be more glorious if you are seen to have made a martyr of an adulteress. than to have made again an adulteress of a martyr."

33. What do you think was the end? The two contended, and both gained the victory, and the crown was not divided, but became two. So the holy martyrs, conferring benefits one on the other, gave the one the impulse and the other the result to their martyrdom.

CHAPTER V.

The story of the two Pythagorean friends, Damon and Pythias, is related by St. Ambrose, who points out that the case mentioned in the last chapter is more praiseworthy. A comparison is instituted between the treatment of their gods by heathen without any punishment, and Jeroboam's irreverence with its punishment.

34. AND the schools of the philosophers laud Damon and Pythias—the Pythagoreans—to the skies, of whom one, when condemned to death, asked for time to set his affairs in order, whereupon, the tyrant, in his cunning, not supposing that such could be found, asked for a bondsman who should suffer the penalty if the other delayed his return. I do not know which act of the two was the more noble. The one found the bondsman, the other offered himself. And so while he who was condemned met with some delay, the bondsman with calm countenance did not refuse death. As he was being led forth his friend returned, and offered his neck to the axe. Then the tyrant, wondering that friendship was dearer to philosophers than life, asked himself to be received into friendship by those whom he had condemned. The grace of Virtue was so great that it moved even a tyrant.

35. These things are worthy of praise; but are inferior to our instance. For those two were men, with us one was a virgin, who had first to be superior to her sex; those were friends, these were unknown to each other; those offered themselves to one tyrant, these to many tyrants; and these more cruel, for in the former case the tyrant spared them, these slew them; with the former one was bound by necessity, with these the will of each was free. In this, too, the latter were the wiser, that with those the end of their

zeal was the pleasure of friendship, with these the crown of martyrdom, for they strove for men, these for God.

36. And since we have mentioned that man who was condemned, it is fitting to add what he thought of his gods, that you may judge how weak they are whom their own followers deride. For he, having come into the temple of Jupiter, bade them take off the fillet of gold with which his image was crowned, and to put on one of wool instead, saying that the golden fillet was cold in winter and heavy in summer. So he derided his god as being unable to bear either a weight or cold. He, too, when he saw the golden beard of Æsculapius, bade them remove it, saying that it was not fit for the son to have a beard when the father had none. Again, he took away the golden bowls from the images which held them, saying that he ought to receive what the gods gave. For, said he, men make prayers to receive good things from the gods, and nothing is better than gold; if, however, gold be evil, the gods ought not to have it; if it be good, it is better that men should have it who know how to use it.

37. Such objects of ridicule were they, that neither could Jupiter defend his garment, nor Æsculapius his beard, for Apollo had not yet begun to grow one; nor could all those who are esteemed gods keep the golden bowls which they were holding, not fearing the charge of theft so much as not having any feeling. Who, then, would worship them, who can neither defend themselves as gods nor hide themselves as men?

38. But when in the temple of our God, that wicked king Jeroboam took away the gifts which his father had laid

up, and offered to idols upon the holy altar, did not his right hand, which he stretched out, wither, and his idols, which he called upon, were not able to help him? Then, turning to the Lord, he asked for pardon, and at once his hand which had withered by sacrilege was healed by true religion. So complete an example was there set forth in one person, both of divine mercy and wrath when he who was sacrificing suddenly lost his right hand, but when penitent received forgiveness.

CHAPTER VI.

St. Ambrose, in concluding the second book, ascribes any good there may be in it to the merits of the virgins, and sets forth that it was right before laying down any severe precepts to encourage them by examples, as is done both in human teaching and in holy Scripture.

39. I, WHO have been not yet three years a bishop, have prepared this offering for you, holy virgins, although untaught by my own experience, yet having learnt much from your mode of life. For what experience could have grown up in so short a time of being initiated in religion? If you find any flowers herein, gather them together in the bosom of your lives. These are not precepts for virgins, but instances taken from virgins. My words have sketched the likeness of your virtue, you may see the reflection of your gravity, as it were, in the mirror of this discourse. If you have received any pleasure from my ability, all the fragrance of this book is yours. And since there are as many opinions as there are persons, if there be anything simple in my treatise let all read it; if anything stronger, let the more mature prove it; if anything modest, let it cleave to the breast and tinge the cheeks; if there be anything flowery, let the flowery age of youth not disdain it.

40. We ought to stir up the love of the bride, for it is written: "Thou shalt love the Lord thy God." At bridal feasts we ought to adorn the hair at least with some ornaments of prayer, for it is written: "Smite the hands together, and strike with the foot." We ought to scatter roses on those uninterrupted bridals. Even in these temporal marriages the bride is received with acclamation before she receives commands, lest hard commands

should hurt her, before love cherished by kindness grows strong.

41. Horses learn to love the sound of patting their necks, that they may not refuse the yoke, and are first trained with words of enticement before the stripe of discipline. But when the horse has submitted its neck to the yoke, the rein pulls in, and the spur urges on, and its companions draw it, and the driver bids it. So, too, our virgin ought first to play with pious love, and admire the golden supports of the heavenly marriage couch on the very threshold of marriage, and to see the door-posts adorned with wreaths of leaves, and to taste the delight of the musicians playing within; that she may not through fear withdraw herself from the Lord's yoke, before she obeys His call.

42. "Come, then, hither from Lebanon, My spouse, come hither from Lebanon, thou shalt pass and pass through." This verse must be often repeated by us, that at least being called by the words of the Lord, she may follow if there be any who will not trust the words of man. We have not formed this power for ourselves, but have received it; this is the heavenly teaching of the mystic song: "Let Him kiss me with the kisses of His mouth, for Thy breasts are better than wine, and the odor of Thy ointments is above all spices. Thy name is as ointment poured forth." The whole of that place of delights sounds of sport, stirs up approval, calls forth love. "Therefore," it continues, "have the maidens loved Thee and have drawn Thee, let us run after the odor of Thy ointments. The King hath brought me into His chamber." She began with kisses, and so attained to the chamber.

43. She, now so patient of hard toil, and of practiced virtue, as to open the bars with her hand, go forth into the field, and abide in strongholds, at the beginning ran after the odor of the ointment; soon when she is come into the chamber the ointment is changed. And see whither she goes: "If it be a wall," it is said, "we will build upon it towers of silver." She who sported with kisses now
builds towers that, encircled with the precious battlements of the saints, she may not only render fruitless the attacks of the enemy, but also erect the safe defenses of holy merits.

BOOK III.

CHAPTER I.

St. Ambrose now goes back to the address of Liberius when he gave the veil to Marcellina. Touching on the crowds pressing to the bridal feast of that Spouse Who feeds them all, he passes on to the fitness of her profession on the day on which Christ was born of a Virgin, and concludes with a fervent exhortation to love Him.

1. INASMUCH as I have digressed in what I have said in the two former hooks, it is now time, holy sister, to reconsider those precepts of Liberius of blessed memory which you used to talk over with me, as the holier the man the more pleasing is his discourse. For he, when on the Nativity of the Savior in the Church of St. Peter you signified your profession of virginity by your change of attire (and what day could be better than that on which the Virgin received her child?) whilst many virgins were standing round and vying with each other for your companionship. "You," said he, "my daughter, have desired a good espousal. You see how great a crowd has come together for the birthday of your Spouse, and none has gone away without food. This is He, Who, when invited to the marriage feast, changed water into wine. He, too, will confer the pure sacrament of virginity on you who before were subject to the vile elements of material nature. This is He Who fed four thousand in the wilderness with five loaves and two fishes." He could have fed more; if more had been there to be fed, they would have been. And now He has called many to your espousal, but it is not now barley bread, but the Body from heaven which is supplied.

2. To-day, indeed, He was born after the manner of men, of a Virgin, but was begotten of the Father before all things, resembling His mother in body, His Father in power. Only-begotten on earth, and Only-begotten in heaven. God of God, born of a Virgin, Righteousness from the Father, Power from the Mighty One, Light of Light, not unequal to His Father; nor separated in power, not confused by extension of the Word or enlargement as though mingled with the Father, but distinguished from the Father by virtue of His generation. He is your Brother, without Whom neither things in heaven, nor things in the sea, nor things on earth consist. The good Word of the Father, Which was, it is said, "in the beginning," here you have His eternity. "And," it is said, "the Word was with God." Here you have His power, undivided and inseparable from the Father. "And the Word was God." Here you have His unbegotten Godhead, for your faith is to be drawn from the mutual relationship.

3. Love him, my daughter, for He is good. For, "None is good save God only." For if there be no doubt that the Son is God, and that God is good, there is certainly no doubt that God the Son is good. Love Him I say. He it is Whom the Father begat before the morning star, as being eternal, He brought Him forth from the womb as the Son; He uttered him from His heart, as the Word. He it is in Whom the Father is well pleased; He is the Arm of the Father, for He is Creator of all, and the Wisdom of the Father, for He proceeded from the mouth of God; the Power of the Father, because the fullness of the Godhead dwelled in Him bodily. And the Father so loved Him, as to bear Him in His bosom, and place Him at His right hand, that you may learn His wisdom, and know His power.

4. If, then, Christ is the Power of God, was God ever without power? Was the Father ever without the Son? If the Father of a certainty always was, of a certainty the Son always was. So He is the perfect Son of a perfect Father. For he who derogates from the power, derogates from Him Whose is the power. The Perfection of the Godhead does not admit of inequality. Love, then, Him Whom the Father loves, honor Him Whom the Father honors, for "he that honored not the Son, honored not the Father," and "whoso denies the Son, hath not the Father." So much as to the faith.

CHAPTER II.

Touching next upon the training of a virgin, he speaks of moderation in food and drink, and of restraint upon the impulses of the mind, introducing some teaching upon the fable of the death and resurrection of Hippolytus, and advises the avoidance of certain meats.

5. BUT sometimes even when faith is to be relied upon, youth is not trusted. Use wine, therefore, sparingly, in order that the weakness of the body may not increase, not for pleasurable excitement, for each alike kindles a flame, both wine and youth. Let fasts also put a bridle on tender age, and spare diet restrain the unsubdued appetites with a kind of rein. Let reason check, hope subdue, and fear curb them. For he who knows not how to govern his desires, like a man run away with by wild horses, is overthrown, bruised, torn, and injured.

6. And this is said to have happened to a youth for his love of Diana. But the fable is colored with poet's tales, that Neptune, stirred with grief at his rival being preferred, sent madness upon his horses, whereby his great power might be set forth in that he overcame the youth, not by strength, but by fraud. And from this event a yearly sacrifice is celebrated for Diana, when a horse is offered at her altar. And they say that she was a virgin, and (of which even harlots would be ashamed) yet
could love one who did not love her. But as far as I am concerned let their fables have authority, for though each be criminal, it is yet a less evil that a youth should have been so enamored of an adulteress as to perish, than that two gods should, as they relate, contend for committing adultery, and that Jupiter avenged the grief of his daughter who played the harlot on the physician who cured the

wound of him who had violated Diana in the woods, a most excellent huntress, no doubt, not of wild beasts, but of lust: yet also of wild beasts, so that she was worshipped naked.

7. Let them ascribe, then, to Neptune the mastery over madness, in order to fix on him the crime of unchaste love. Let them ascribe to Diana the rule over the woods, wherein she dwelt, so as to establish the adultery which she practiced. Let them ascribe to Æsculapius the restoration of the dead so long as they confess that when struck by lightning he himself escaped not. Let them also ascribe to Jupiter the thunderbolts which he did not possess, so that they witness to the disgrace with which he was laden.

8. And I think that one should sparingly eat all kinds of food which cause heat to the limbs, for flesh drags down even eagles as they fly. But within you let that bird of which we read, "Thy youth shall be renewed like the eagle's," holding its course on high, swift in its virgin flight, be ignorant of the desire for unnecessary food. The gathering of banquets and salutations must be avoided.

CHAPTER III.

Virgins are exhorted to avoid visits, to observe modesty, to be silent during the celebration of the Mysteries after the example of Mary. Then after narrating the story of a heathen youth, and saying of a poet, St. Ambrose relates a miracle wrought by a holy priest.

9. I WILL, too, that visits amongst the younger, except such as may be due to parents and those of like age, be few. For modesty is worn away by intercourse, and boldness breaks forth, laughter creeps in, and bashfulness is lessened, whilst politeness is studied. Not to answer one who asks a question is childishness, to answer is nonsense. I should prefer, therefore, that conversation should rather be wanting to a virgin, than abound. For if women are bidden to keep silence in churches, even about divine things, and to ask their husbands at home, what do we think should be the caution of virgins, in whom modesty adorns their age, and silence commends their modesty.

10. Was it a small sign of modesty that when Rebecca came to wed Isaac, and saw her bridegroom, she took a veil, that she might not be seen before they were united? Certainly the fair virgin feared not for her beauty, but for her modesty. What of Rachel, how she, when Jacob's kiss had been taken, wept and groaned, and would not have ceased weeping had she not known him to be a kinsman? So she both observed what was due to modesty, and omitted not kindly affection. But if it is said to a man: "Gaze not on a maid, lest she cause thee to fall," what is to be said to a consecrated virgin, who, if she loves, sins in mind; if she is loved, in act also?

11. The virtue of silence, especially in Church, is very great. Let no sentence of the divine lessons escape you; if you give ear, restrain your voice, utter no word with your lips which you would wish to recall, but let your boldness to speak be sparing. For in truth in much speaking there is abundance of sin. To the murderer it was said: "Thou hast sinned, be silent," that he might not sin more; but to the virgin it must be said, "Be silent lest thou sin." For Mary, as we read, kept in heart all things that were said concerning her Son, and do you, when any passage is read where Christ is announced as about to come, or is shown to have come, not make a noise by talking, but attend. Is anything more unbecoming than the divine words should be so drowned by talking, as not to be heard, believed, or made known, that the sacraments should be indistinctly heard through the sound of voices, that prayer should be hindered when offered for the salvation of all?

12. The Gentiles pay respect to their idols by silence, of which this instance is given: As Alexander, the king of the Macedonians, was sacrificing, the sleeve of a barbarian lad who was lighting the lamp for him caught fire and burnt his body, yet he remained without moving and neither betrayed the pain by a groan, nor showed his suffering by silent tears. Such was the discipline of reverence in a barbarian lad that nature was subdued. Yet he feared not the gods, who were no gods, but the king. For why should he fear those who if the same fire had caught them would have burnt?

13. How much better still is it where a youth at his father's banquet is bidden not to betray by coarse gestures his unchaste loves. And do you, holy virgin, abstain from

groans, cries, coughing, and laughter at the Mystery. Can you not at the Mystery do what he did at a banquet? Let virginity be first marked by the voice, let modesty close the mouth, let religion remove weakness, and habit instruct nature. Let her gravity first announce a virgin to me, a modest approach, a sober gait, a bashful countenance, and let the march of virtue be preceded by the evidence of integrity. That virgin is not sufficiently worthy of approval who has to be enquired about when she is seen.

14. There is common story how, when the excessive croaking of frogs was resounding in the ears of the faithful people, the priest of God bade them be silent, and show reverence to the sacred words, and then at once the noise was stilled. Shall then the marshes keep silence and not the frogs? And shall irrational animals re-acknowledge by reverence what they know not by nature? While the shamelessness of men is such, that many care not to pay that respect to the religious feelings of their minds, which they do to the pleasure of their ears.

CHAPTER IV.

Having summed up the address of Liberius, St. Ambrose passes on to the virtues of his sister, especially her fasts, which however he advises her to moderate to some extent, and to exercise herself in other matters, after the example which he adduces. Especially he recommends the Lord's Prayer, and the repetition of Psalms by night, and the recitation of the Creed before daylight.

15. AFTER such a fashion did Liberius of holy memory address you, in words beyond the reality of practice in most cases, but coming short of your performance, who have not only attained to the whole of discipline by your virtue, but have surpassed it in your zeal. For we are bidden to practice fasting, but only for single days; but you, multiplying nights and days, pass untold periods without food, and if ever requested to partake of some, and to lay aside your book a little while, you at once answer: "Man doth not live by bread alone, but by every word of God." Your very meals consisted but of what food came to hand, so that fasting is to be preferred to eating what was repugnant; your drink is from the spring, your weeping and prayer combine, your sleep is on your book.

16. These kings were suited to younger years, whilst he was ripening with the gray hairs of age; but when a virgin has gained the triumph over her subdued body, she should lessen her toil, that she may be preserved as teacher for a younger age. The vine laden with the fruitful branches of full growth soon breaks unless it be from time to time kept back. But whilst it is young let it grow rank, and as it grows older be pruned, so as not to grow into a forest of twigs, or die deprived of life by its exceptive produce. A good husbandman by tending the soil keeps the vine in

excellent order, protects it from cold, and guards it from being parched by the mid-day sun. And he works his land by turns, or if he will not let it lie fallow, he alternates his crops, so that the fields may rest through change of produce. Do you too, a veteran in virginity, at least sow the fields of your breast with different seeds, at one time with moderate sustenance, at another with sparing fasts, with reading, work, and prayer, that change of toil may be as a truce for rest.

17. The whole land does not produce the same harvest. On one side vines grow on the hills, on another you can see the purple olives, elsewhere the scented roses. And after leaving the plough, the strong husbandman with his fingers scrapes the soil to plant the roots of flowers, and with the rough hands wherewith he turns the bullocks striving amongst the vines, he gently presses the udders of the sheep. The land is the better the more numerous are its fruits. So do you, following the example of a good husbandman, avoid cleaving your soil with perpetual fasting as if with deep ploughings. Let the rose of modesty bloom in your garden, and the lily of the mind, and let the violet beds drink from the source of sacred blood. There is a common saying, "What you wish to perform abundantly, sometimes do not do at all." There ought to be something to add to the days of Lent, but so that nothing be done for the sake of ostentation, but of religion.

18. Frequent prayer also commends us to God. For if the prophet says, "Seven times a day have I praised Thee,"[3280] though he was busy with the affairs of a kingdom, what ought we to do, who read: "Watch and pray that ye enter

not into temptation"? Certainly our customary prayers ought to be said with giving of thanks, when we rise from sleep, when we go forth, when we prepare to receive food, after receiving it, and at the hour of incense, when at last we are going to rest.

19. And again in your bed-chamber itself, I would have you join psalms in frequent interchange with the Lord's prayer, either when you wake up, or before sleep bedews your body, so that at the very commencement of rest sleep may find you free from the care of worldly matters, meditating upon the things of God. And, indeed, he who first found out the name of Philosophy itself, every day before he went to rest, had the flute-player play softer melodies to soothe his mind disturbed by worldly cares. But he, like a man washing tiles, fruitlessly desired to drive away worldly things by worldly means, for he was, indeed, rather besmearing himself with fresh mud, in seeking a reward from pleasure, but let us, having wiped off the filth of earthly vices, purify our utmost souls from every defilement of the flesh.

20. We ought, also, especially to repeat the Creed, as a seal upon our hearts, daily, before light, and to recur to it in thought whenever we are in fear of anything. For when is the soldier in his tent or the warrior in battle without his military oath?

CHAPTER V.

St. Ambrose, speaking of tears, explains David's saying, "Every night wash I my couch with my tears," and goes on to speak of Christ bearing our griefs and infirmities. Everything should be referred to His honor, and we ought to rejoice with spiritual joy, but not after a worldly fashion.

21. AND who can now fail to understand that the holy prophet said for our instruction: "Every night will I wash my couch and water my bed with my tears"? For if you take it literally for his bed, he shows that such abundance of tears should be shed as to wash the bed and water it with tears, the couch of him who is praying, for weeping has to do with the present, rewards with the future, since it is said: "Blessed are ye that weep, for ye shall laugh;" or if we take the word of the prophet as applied to our bodies, we must wash away the offences of the body with tears of penitence. For Solomon made himself a bed of wood from Lebanon, its pillars were of silver, its bottom of gold, its back strewn with gems. What is that bed but the fashion of our body? For by gems is set forth the splendor of the brightness of the air, fire is set forth by the gold, water by silver, and earth by wood, of which four elements the human body consists, in which our soul rests, if it do not exist deprived of rest by the roughness of hills or the damp ground, but raised on high, above vices, supported by the wood. For which reason David also says: "The Lord will send him help upon his bed of pain."[3287] For how can that be a bed of pain which cannot feel pain, and which has no feeling? But the body of pain is like the body of that death, of which it is said: "O wretched man that I am, who shall deliver me from the body of this death?"

22. And since I have inserted a clause in which mention is made of the Lord's Body, lest anyone should be troubled at reading that the Lord took a body of pain, let him remember that the Lord grieved and wept over the death of Lazarus, and was wounded in His passion, and that from the wound there went forth blood and water, and that He gave up His Spirit. Water for washing, Blood for drink, the Spirit for His rising again. For Christ alone is to us hope, faith, and love—hope in His resurrection, faith in the laver, and love in the sacrament.

23. And as He took a body of pain, so too He turned His bed in His weakness, for He converted it to the benefit of human flesh. For by His Passion weakness was ended, and death by His resurrection. And yet you ought to mourn for the world but to rejoice in the Lord, to be sad for penitence but joyful for grace, though, too, the teacher of the Gentiles by a wholesome precept has bidden to weep with them that weep, and to rejoice with them that do rejoice.

24. But let him who desires to solve the whole difficulty of this question have recourse to the same Apostle. "Whatsoever ye do," says he, "in word or deed, do all in the Name of our Lord Jesus Christ, giving thanks to God the Father by Him." Let us then refer all our words and deeds to Christ, Who brought life out of death, and created light out of darkness. For as a sick body is at one time cherished by warmth, at another soothed by cool applications, and the variation of remedies, if carried out according to the direction of the physician, is healthful, but if done in opposition to his orders increases the

sickness; so whatever is paid to Christ is a remedy, whatever is done by our own will is harmful.

25. There ought then to be the joy of the mind, conscious of right, not excited by unrestrained feasts, or nuptial concerts, for in such modesty is not safe, and temptation may be suspected where excessive dancing accompanies festivities. I desire that the virgins of God should be far from this. For as a certain teacher of this world has said: "No one dances when sober unless he is mad." Now if, according to the wisdom of this world, either drunkenness or madness is the cause of dancing, what a warning is given to us amongst the instances mentioned in the Divine Scriptures, where John, the forerunner of Christ, being beheaded at the wish of a dancer, is an instance that the allurements of dancing did more harm than the madness of sacrilegious anger.

CHAPTER VI.

Having mentioned the Baptist, St. Ambrose enters into a description of the events concerning his
death, and speaks against dancing and the festivities of the wicked.

26. AND since we must not cursorily pass by the mention of so great a man, let us consider who he was, by whom, on what account, how, and at what time he was slain. A just man, he is put to death by adulterers, and the penalty of a capital crime is turned off by the guilty on to the judge. Again the reward of the dancer is the death of the prophet. Lastly (a matter of honor even to all barbarians), the cruel sentence is given in the midst of banqueting and festivities, and the news of the deadly crime is carried from the banquet to the prison, and then from the prison to the banquet. How many crimes are there in one wicked act!

27. A banquet of death is set out with royal luxury, and when a larger concourse than usual had come together, the daughter of the queen, sent for from within the private apartments, is brought forth to dance in the sight of men. What could she have learnt from an adulteress but loss of modesty? Is anything so conducive to lust as with unseemly movements thus to expose in nakedness those
parts of the body which either nature has hidden or custom has veiled, to sport with the looks, to turn the neck, to loosen the hair? Fitly was the next step an offence against God. For what modesty can there be where there is dancing and noise and clapping of hands?

28. "Then," it is said, "the king being pleased, said unto the damsel, that she should ask of the king whatsoever she

would. Then he swore that if she asked he would give her even the half of his kingdom." See how worldly men themselves judge of their worldly power, so as to give even kingdoms for dancing. But the damsel, being taught by her mother, demanded that the head of John should be brought to her on a dish. That which is said that "the king was sorry," is not repentance on the part of the king, but a confession of guilt, which is, according to the wont of the divine rule, that they who have done evil condemn themselves by their own confession. "But for their sakes which sat with him," it is said. What is more base than that a murder should be committed in order not to displease those who sat at meat? "And," it follows, "for his oath's sake." What a new religion!

www.ingramcontent.com/pod-product-compliance
Lightning Source LLC
Chambersburg PA
CBHW052113070526
44584CB00017B/2459